BETTER–*than* YESTERDAY

PROVERBS OF A WOMAN'S HEART

WORKBOOK

By

VICKI L. KEMP

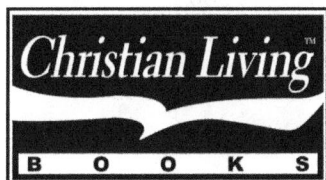

Christian Living Books, Inc.
P. O. Box 7584
Largo, MD 20792
christianlivingbooks.com
We bring your dreams to fruition.

ISBN 9781562293598

Printed in the United States of America

CONTENTS

Proverb One: A Challenge to Forgive and Love 2

Proverb Two: Let Go to Live 4

Proverb Three: A Kingdom Woman 6

Proverb Four: Unlimited Possibilities 8

Proverb Five: Love You – Still 10

Proverb Six: Rejection 12

Proverb Seven: Negativity Breeds an Untamed Mindset 14

Proverb Eight: I'm Right. They're Wrong 16

Proverb Nine: God's Peace 18

Proverb Ten: Sisterhood, a Village 20

Proverb Eleven: A Constant Friend 22

Proverb Twelve: Laugh in His Face 24

Proverb Thirteen: Beauty, Brains, and Favor 26

Proverb Fourteen: It's as Cruel as the Grave – Jealousy 28

Proverb Fifteen: The Catalyst of Pride Is I 30

Proverb Sixteen: My Kingdom Man 32

Proverbs Seventeen: That Other Kind of Man 34

Proverb Eighteen: Safe, Secure, and Settled 36

Proverb Nineteen: You See My Flaws, but God Sees Differently 38

Proverb Twenty: I Am Greater than FEAR 40

Proverb Twenty-One: Never too Late to Be Free 42

Proverb Twenty-Two: To Honor Her Is the Greatest Joy 44

Proverb Twenty-Three: The Absolute Truth 46

Proverb Twenty-Four: Silence 48

Proverb Twenty-Five: Givers and Takers 50

Proverb Twenty-Six: Write Your Story 52

INTRODUCTION

The enemy works hard to keep us ineffective and bound by thoughts, emotions and past experiences. It is my prayer that this workbook would serve as a powerful tool to help you take a deeper look at life and living. I've challenged you to read the compilation of proverbs in *Better than Yesterday*; now, I challenge you to do the work. I desire that you take time to answer each challenge, carefully and honestly. Take a stand and don't allow the designs of the enemy to keep you stuck in your yesterday.

We all have struggles that we continually fight to overcome. As stated in *Better than Yesterday*, I've learned that the ultimate reward for defeating the struggle is the chance – the matchless opportunity to live without strongholds and in complete freedom. The goal is to remain free. Abundantly free. With God, you are far better than any past failures or hang-ups. Through faith in God, see yourself free.

The Workbook Challenge

- Study each **Challenge** in order. It is best that you not move ahead
- Dissect and meditate on its insights
- Challenge yourself to complete each question in truth and transparency
- Go deeper into the material by completing the **Key Thoughts**
- Be honest with yourself and ask God to go up to the attic of your mind and down to the basement of your soul and uncover areas that are dormant and hiding
- Be creative and transparent
- Write your own Proverb similar to those in *Better than Yesterday* using the prompts provided.

At the end of each proverb, meditate on at least three **Kingdom Words** which will empower you to be better and triumphant. For example, my words are Peace, Wholeness and God's Favor. Be mindful that your words have the power to make or break you; therefore, speak words of positivity over your life and also into your situations. Kingdom words, which are God's words, produce success and progress. Spend time studying and meditating on the **Checkpoints** at the end of each Challenge. The word empowers us to not only be better but victorious. So, open your heart to God as you ask Him to change your perception of life and living. When you complete each challenge, you will see yourself better, by faith. Declare that you are whole and today is a new and better day.

Refuse to be tied to the lies and tricks of the enemy. Our great God is a genius over every plan plotted against us. Satan has deceived us for too long; we dare not continue to let him rob us of the freedom God promised in His Word! It is never too late to see yourself free through the eyes of faith.

Many are struggling, even in the church, although they are consistently hearing the Word. The struggle may seem unbearable because they have not challenged or applied truths to better their lives. This workbook will help you think before you respond to the designs of the enemy – fiercely and confidently. By faith, you are better – more than better – than yesterday.

Connect with Lady Kemp

Twitter	@LadyVKemp	IG	LadyVickiLKemp
Facebook	Vicki Kemp	Website	vickilynnekemp.com
Business Email	Kempvicki@aol.com		

Sign up for my weekly motivational email list at uarebetterthanyesterday@gmail.com.

PROVERB ONE
A CHALLENGE to FORGIVE and LOVE

Thoughts to Ponder

Imagine standing before your Lord and Savior, Jesus Christ, and being asked, "Did you forgive those that hurt you and caused you pain?" What would your answer be? We live a life to live again. We do not want past struggles to detour us from eternal life in Heaven. Unforgiveness is not worth you missing your promise. To forgive and love is better.

The Challenge

1. Write down the names of the people, including yourself, you need to forgive and why.

_____
_____
_____
_____

2. At times, relationships suffer when we feel that our past situations are insurmountable. Please explain.

_____
_____
_____
_____

3. Expound on this statement: You can experience pure freedom if you are willing to deal with the posture of your heart.

_____
_____
_____

4. Has unforgiveness ever caused you to be reckless?

_____
_____
_____

5. How did you overcome this behavior?

_____
_____
_____

Key Thoughts

6. **Define unforgiveness from your understanding and explain how it has been playing a part in your life?**

_____

_____

_____

_____

_____

7. **Write your own story using this prompt: I have held on to grudges, bitterness and unforgiveness because**

_____

_____

_____

_____

_____

Kingdom Words

Write three kingdom words that will empower you to be better, victorious and triumphant in relation to this proverb.

1. _____

2. _____

3. _____

Check Points

Let all bitterness, and wrath, and anger, and clamour, and evil speaking, be put away from you, with all malice: And be ye kind one to another, tenderhearted, forgiving one another, even as God for Christ's sake hath forgiven you. (Eph. 4:31-32)

For if ye forgive men their trespasses, your heavenly Father will also forgive you. (Matthew 6:14)

Judge not, and ye shall not be judged: condemn not, and ye shall not be condemned: forgive, and ye shall be forgiven. (Luke 6:37)

And when ye stand praying, forgive, if ye have ought against any: that your Father also which is in heaven may forgive you your trespasses. (Mark 11:25)

Dearly beloved, avenge not yourselves, but rather give place unto wrath: for it is written, Vengeance is mine; I will repay, saith the Lord. Therefore if thine enemy hunger, feed him; if he thirst, give him drink: for in so doing thou shalt heap coals of fire on his head. Be not overcome by evil, but overcome evil with good. (Romans 12:19-21)

But I say unto you, Love your enemies, bless them that curse you, do good to them that hate you, and pray for them which despitefully use you, and persecute you; That ye may be the children of your Father which is in heaven: for he maketh his sun to rise on the evil and on the good, and sendeth rain on the just and on the unjust. (Matthew 5:44-45)

Put on therefore, as the elect of God, holy and beloved, bowels of mercies, kindness, humbleness of mind, meekness, longsuffering; Forbearing one another, and forgiving one another, if any man have a quarrel against any: even as Christ forgave you, so also do ye. (Colossians 3:12-13)

LET GO to LIVE

Thoughts to Ponder

Take a deep breath and think. You are still here. You are yet in the land of the living. You survived the very thing that was designed to stop you. Then, rejoice and keep moving forward. Let it all go and live. Life is beautiful when you are free to live without handcuffs on. We remain in handcuffs when we allow others to dictate our freedom.

The Challenge

1. Write down any past hurts that continue to tug at your heart. How have they become emotional security blankets for you?

   _____
   _____
   _____

2. What do you need to release in order to grow? Be specific. Write it down.

   _____
   _____
   _____

3. Explain how you have remained in denial due to past pain. What have you refused to let go of because you felt justified in holding onto your pain?

   _____
   _____
   _____

4. What is your definition of letting go and has your definition worked for you?

   _____
   _____
   _____

5. Do you believe that letting go paves the way for future triumph? Explain.

   _____
   _____
   _____

6. What does it mean to you to live?

_____

_____

_____

_____

_____

7. Write your own story using this prompt: Life is amazing when you choose to release

_____

_____

_____

_____

_____

Kingdom Words

Write three kingdom words that will empower you to be better, victorious and triumphant in relation to this proverb.

1. _____

2. _____

3. _____

Check Points

He brought me up also out of a horrible pit, out of the miry clay, and set my feet upon a rock, and established my goings. And he hath put a new song in my mouth, even praise unto our God: many shall see it, and fear, and shall trust in the Lord. (Psalms 40:2-3)

A new heart also will I give you, and a new spirit will I put within you: and I will take away the stony heart out of your flesh, and I will give you a heart of flesh. (Ezekiel 36:26)

Be angry and do not sin; do not let the sun go down on your anger, and give no opportunity to the devil. (Ephesians 4:26-27 ESV)

Little children, let us not love in word or talk but indeed and in truth. (1 John 3:18 ESV)

Let us not therefore judge one another anymore: but judge this rather, that no man put a stumbling block or an occasion to fall in his brother's way. (Romans 14:13)

Let us therefore follow after the things which make for peace, and things wherewith one may edify another. (Romans 14:19)

And let us consider one another to provoke unto love and to good works: Not forsaking the assembling of ourselves together, as the manner of some is; but exhorting one another: and so much the more, as ye see the day approaching. (Hebrew 10: 24-25)

Truly my soul waiteth upon God: from him cometh my salvation. He only is my rock and my salvation; he is my defense; I shall not be greatly moved. (Psalms 62:1-2)

PROVERB THREE
A KINGDOM WOMAN

Thoughts to Ponder

See yourself better no matter how the enemy attempts to tamper with your mind and emotions. Remind him that you have authority over any and all mind games. You are a kingdom woman. You are a woman of value and strength. Wisdom is birthed from your life experiences. You are a gift on the earth. You sit in queenly places.

The Challenge

1. What past struggles have challenged your confidence? Explain the necessary steps you will take to build your confidence.

_____

_____

_____

2. What hindrances are you currently facing which stop you from moving forward and becoming a better you? Evaluate why.

_____

_____

_____

3. How have you allowed other's words to frame your self-image or self-esteem?

_____

_____

_____

4. Have women allowed stereotypes to define who they should be? Give examples.

_____

_____

_____

5. "Be angry, and yet do not sin; do not let the sun go down on your anger" (Ephesians 4:26 NASB). Reflect on that scripture. Have you ever felt the right to be angry when others have challenged your character? Please explain.

_____

_____

_____

6. **What does it mean to be a woman of value?**

_____
_____
_____
_____
_____

7. **Write your own story using this prompt: I am not who I used to be. I am a kingdom woman, and I declare**

_____
_____
_____
_____
_____

Kingdom Words

Write three kingdom words that will empower you to be better, victorious and triumphant in relation to this proverb.

1. _____
2. _____
3. _____

Check Points

For we are his workmanship, created in Christ Jesus unto good works, which God hath before ordained that we should walk in them. (Ephesians 2:10)

But ye are a chosen generation, a royal priesthood, an holy nation, a peculiar people; that ye should shew forth the praises of him who hath called you out of darkness into his marvellous light. (1 Peter 2:9)

Now unto him that is able to keep you from falling, and to present you faultless before the presence of his glory with exceeding joy, To the only wise God our Saviour, be glory and majesty, dominion and power, both now and ever. Amen. (Jude 24:25)

Thus you were adorned with gold and silver, and your dress was of fine linen, silk and embroidered cloth You ate fine flour, honey and oil; so you were exceedingly beautiful and advanced to royalty. (Ezekiel 16:13 NASB)

And the Lord shall make thee the head, and not the tail; and thou shalt be above only, and thou shalt not be beneath; if that thou hearken unto the commandments of the Lord thy God, which I command thee this day, to observe and to do them. (Deuteronomy 28:13)

Let this mind be in you, which was also in Christ Jesus. (Philippians 2:5)

For you have been born again [that is, reborn from above—spiritually transformed, renewed, and set apart for His purpose] not of seed which is perishable but [from that which is] imperishable and immortal, that is, through the living and everlasting word of God. (1 Peter 1:23 AMP)

UNLIMITED POSSIBILITIES

Thoughts to Ponder

You can have what you desire to have. Believe by faith and speak that desire into existence. Your voice is powerful and it holds vibration in the earth for it reaches in the heavenlies when your words are backed by faith. All that you aspire to be, that is who you are by faith. All that you aim to do, it's done by faith. Believe. Speak it and watch each goal and task come to past.

The Challenge

1. **What has distracted you from achieving your God-given dreams?**

   _____

   _____

   _____

   _____

2. **Find a scripture that encourages you to release the God-given passion that will encourage you to succeed in life. Using the scripture, write a confession. Revisit it daily.**

   _____

   _____

   _____

   _____

3. **Dig deep; describe past regrets due to procrastinating. How will you manage differently in the future that will cause you to be successful?**

   _____

   _____

   _____

   _____

4. **Do you have a present fear of being successful? Does a fear of failure cause you not to accomplish your dreams? Please explain.**

   _____

   _____

   _____

   _____

5. Unlimited possibilities are going beyond expectations. How does this relate to your life?

_____
_____
_____
_____
_____

6. Write your own story using this prompt: I will not allow anything or anyone to hold me back from

_____
_____
_____
_____
_____

Kingdom Words

Write three kingdom words that will empower you to be better, victorious and triumphant in relation to this proverb.

1. _____
2. _____
3. _____

Check Points

You, dear children, are from God and have overcome them, because the one who is in you is greater than the one who is in the world. (1 John 4:4 NIV)

But my God shall supply all your need according to his riches in glory by Christ Jesus. (Philippians 4:19)

I can do all things through Christ which strengtheneth me. (Philippians 4:13)

But be ye doers of the word, and not hearers only, deceiving your own selves. (James 1:22)

Strengthened with all might, according to his glorious power, unto all patience and longsuffering with joyfulness. (Colossians 1:11)

Rooted and built up in him, and stablished in the faith, as ye have been taught, abounding therein with thanksgiving. (Colossians 2:7)

Therefore I tell you, whatever you ask for in prayer, believe that you have received it, and it will be yours. (Mark 11:24)

Give, and it shall be given unto you; good measure, pressed down, and shaken together, and running over, shall men give into your bosom. For with the same measure that ye mete withal, it shall be measured to you again. (Luke 6:38)

LOVE YOU – STILL

Thoughts to Ponder

It is powerful when you can genuinely love someone who has hurt your heart to the core. Agape love enables you to love beyond the negative. True love allows you to be free. The question is, do you want to be free? Of course, you desire to be free. Why would you remain in bondage? Love is a prevailing weapon against the powers of darkness. See yourself better and love, still.

The Challenge

1. What has hindered you from loving others as the Word commands?

_____

_____

_____

2. Describe times you've felt hurt and abandoned and what step(s) you must take, according to the Word, to walk in victory.

_____

_____

_____

3. Read 1 Corinthians 13:1-13. What attribute of love is missing in your life? Contemplate why.

_____

_____

_____

4. How can you experience true love when you feel mistreated?

_____

_____

_____

5. How can you demonstrate love towards your enemies?

_____

_____

_____

Key Thoughts

6. Here is a sincere question. Allow yourself time to think before answering. Is it difficult to love while in the midst of pain? And how can we reach a place at which we can love genuinely?

_____
_____
_____
_____

7. Write your own story using this prompt: I love you, still, and I will not allow

_____
_____
_____
_____

Kingdom Words

Write three kingdom words that will empower you to be better, victorious and triumphant in relation to this proverb.

1. _____
2. _____
3. _____

Checkpoints

Lie not one to another, seeing that ye have put off the old man with his deeds; And have put on the new man, which is renewed in knowledge after the image of him that created him. (Colossians 3:9-10)

Therefore if any man be in Christ, he is a new creature: old things are passed away; behold, all things are become new. (2 Corinthians 5:17)

In whom the god of this world hath blinded the minds of them which believe not, lest the light of the glorious gospel of Christ, who is the image of God, should shine unto them. (2 Corinthians 4:4)

Charity suffereth long, and is kind; charity envieth not; charity vaunteth not itself, is not puffed up, Doth not behave itself unseemly, seeketh not her own, is not easily provoked, thinketh no evil; Rejoiceth not in iniquity, but rejoiceth in the truth; Beareth all things, believeth all things, hopeth all things, endureth all things. (1 Corinthians 13:4-7)

And let us consider one another to provoke unto love and to good works: Not forsaking the assembling of ourselves together, as the manner of some is; but exhorting one another: and so much the more, as ye see the day approaching. (Hebrews 10:24-25)

Make full my joy, that ye be of the same mind, having the same love, being of one accord, of one mind; doing nothing through faction or through vainglory, but in lowliness of mind each counting other better than himself; 4 not looking each of you to his own things, but each of you also to the things of others. (Philippians 2:2-4 ASV)

Let not mercy and truth forsake thee: bind them about thy neck; write them upon the table of thine heart: So shalt thou find favour and good understanding in the sight of God and man. (Proverbs 3:3-4)

REJECTION

The emotion that was designed to keep you in isolation, is the emotion that will thrust you forward to be a better you. Be an example of kindness and allow yourself to be used to set a woman free that once looked like you.

The Challenge

1. **How has rejection made you feel? Be specific.**

_____

_____

_____

_____

_____

2. **How can you overcome past rejections according to the Word? Explain.**

_____

_____

_____

_____

_____

3. **How long have you allowed yourself to walk in rejection and when did you notice that it held you hostage?**

_____

_____

_____

_____

_____

4. **What has rejection caused you to deal with, secretly?**

_____

_____

_____

_____

_____

Key Thoughts

5. What may have prevented you from seeking help or insight from a trusted friend, family member, or counselor?

_____
_____
_____
_____
_____

6. Write your own story using this prompt: Today is a new day, and I will not allow rejection to

_____
_____
_____
_____
_____

Kingdom Words

Write three kingdom words that will empower you to be better, victorious and triumphant in relation to this proverb.

1. _____

2. _____

3. _____

Checkpoints

Strengthened with all might, according to his glorious power, unto all patience and longsuffering with joyfulness. (Colossians 1:11)

Above all, taking the shield of faith, wherewith ye shall be able to quench all the fiery darts of the wicked. (Ephesians 6:16)

Who hath delivered us from the power of darkness, and hath translated us into the kingdom of his dear Son. (Colossians 1:13)

Be kindly affectioned one to another with brotherly love; in honour preferring one another; Not slothful in business; fervent in spirit; serving the Lord; Rejoicing in hope; patient in tribulation; continuing instant in prayer; Distributing to the necessity of saints; given to hospitality. (Romans 12:10-13)

Submit yourselves therefore to God. Resist the devil, and he will flee from you. (James 4:7)

Blessed are ye, when men shall hate you, and when they shall separate you from their company, and shall reproach you, and cast out your name as evil, for the Son of man's sake. (Luke 6:22)

And whosoever shall not receive you, nor hear your words, when ye depart out of that house or city, shake off the dust of your feet. (Matthew 10:14)

NEGATIVITY BREEDS *an* UNTAMED MINDSET

Thoughts to Ponder

There were times in your life when you were barely hanging on. Negative thoughts dominated your mind. Thank You, Jesus, for amazing grace. You are better for prayer was your ally and Jesus was your strong tower. Never forget that Jesus is your source of strength.

The Challenge

1. How can you take control of your thoughts? What does it mean to be transformed by the renewing of your mind, according to Romans 12:2? Explain.

   _____
   _____
   _____
   _____
   _____

2. Write a confession to defeat the enemy in your mind. Read and meditate on it daily.

   _____
   _____
   _____
   _____
   _____

3. How can you steer clear of the world's logic concerning negativity?

   _____
   _____
   _____
   _____
   _____

4. What positive steps have you taken to release negative thought patterns?

   _____
   _____
   _____
   _____
   _____

Key thoughts

5. **A negative mindset unavoidably causes misery and depression. Please explain.**

_____
_____
_____
_____
_____

6. **Write your own story using this prompt: My mind is renewed by the power of God and**

_____
_____
_____
_____
_____

Kingdom Words

Write three kingdom words that will empower you to be better, victorious and triumphant in relation to this proverb.

1. _____

2. _____

3. _____

Checkpoints

For God hath not given us the spirit of fear; but of power, and of love, and of a sound mind. (2 Timothy 1:7)

Nay, in all these things we are more than conquerors through him that loved us (Romans 8:37)

And they overcame him by the blood of the Lamb, and by the word of their testimony; and they loved not their lives unto the death. (Revelation 12:11)

And these signs shall follow them that believe; In my name shall they cast out devils; they shall speak with new tongues; They shall take up serpents; and if they drink any deadly thing, it shall not hurt them; they shall lay hands on the sick, and they shall recover. (Mark 16:17-18)

For the law of the Spirit of life in Christ Jesus hath made me free from the law of sin and death. (Romans 8:2)

In righteousness shalt thou be established: thou shalt be far from oppression; for thou shalt not fear: and from terror; for it shall not come near thee. (Isaiah 54:14)

Be careful for nothing; but in everything by prayer and supplication with thanksgiving let your requests be made known unto God. And the peace of God, which passeth all understanding, shall keep your hearts and minds through Christ Jesus. Finally, brethren, whatsoever things are true, whatsoever things are honest, whatsoever things are just, whatsoever things are pure, whatsoever things are lovely, whatsoever things are of good report; if there be any virtue, and if there be any praise, think on these things. Those things, which ye have both learned, and received, and heard, and seen in me, do: and the God of peace shall be with you. (Philippians 4:6-9)

I'M RIGHT. THEY'RE WRONG

Thoughts to Ponder

When you realize that God is the Judge, it does not matter who it right or wrong. What matters is what is important to God. Ask yourself the power question: "Who is it that you aim to please?" Your answer should be God; therefore, choose righteousness.

The Challenge

1. **What have you passionately sought to be right about and how did it affect your life?**

_____
_____
_____
_____
_____

2. **What might you consider doing differently should you experience the need to be adamantly right?**

_____
_____
_____
_____
_____

3. **During the most complex confrontations, how will you stay peaceful and guard your character?**

_____
_____
_____
_____
_____

4. **Consider the root of the reason(s) you continue to fight to be right. How you will combat these emotions?**

_____
_____
_____
_____
_____

5. Has your desire to be right caused you to be in negative situations? Please explain the effect it had on your life and the life of others.

_____

_____

_____

_____

_____

_____

6. Write your own story using this prompt: Although I feel that I am right

_____

_____

_____

_____

_____

_____

_____

Kingdom Words

Write three kingdom words that will empower you to be better, victorious and triumphant in relation to this proverb.

1. _____

2. _____

3. _____

Checkpoints

That the God of our Lord Jesus Christ, the Father of glory, may give unto you the spirit of wisdom and revelation in the knowledge of him: The eyes of your understanding being enlightened; that ye may know what is the hope of his calling, and what the riches of the glory of his inheritance in the saints. (Ephesians 1:17-18)

Whoever pursues righteousness and love finds life, prosperity and honor. (Proverbs 21:21 NIV)

Every way of a man is right in his own eyes: but the Lord pondereth the hearts. (Proverbs 21:2)

Blessed *are* they that keep judgment, *and* he that doeth righteousness at all times. (Psalms 106.3)

But seek ye first the kingdom of God, and his righteousness; and all these things shall be added unto you. (Matthew 6:33)

Flee also youthful lusts: but follow righteousness, faith, charity, peace, with them that call on the Lord out of a pure heart. (2 Timothy 2:22)

PROVERB NINE
GOD'S PEACE

Thoughts to Ponder

See, the enemy thought he had the power to steal your peace and keep it. God has all power; therefore, peace is available to you. You have a choice not to allow the enemy to dictate the course of your life. Confront the enemy and take your peace back. Peace is a sweet friend that is a benefit to have around.

The Challenge

1. What have you allowed to steal your peace and caused you not to seek God?

_____
_____
_____
_____
_____

2. What is the meaning of "Thou will keep him in perfect peace, whose mind is stayed on thee: because he trusteth in thee" (Isaiah 26:3)?

_____
_____
_____
_____
_____

3. Have you found it difficult to have peace when you have constantly been disappointed? Explain.

_____
_____
_____
_____
_____

4. What is your explanation for having peace of mind?

_____
_____
_____
_____

Key Thoughts

5. Explain this thought: Peace is being in a state of harmony.

_____
_____
_____
_____
_____
_____
_____

6. Write your own story using this prompt: My peace is not worth

_____
_____
_____
_____
_____
_____
_____
_____

Kingdom Words

Write three kingdom words that will empower you to be better, victorious and triumphant in relation to this proverb.

1. _____

2. _____

3. _____

Checkpoints

Now the Lord of peace himself give you peace always by all means. The Lord be with you all. (2 Thessalonians 3:16)

These things I have spoken unto you, that in me ye might have peace. In the world ye shall have tribulation: but be of good cheer; I have overcome the world. (John 16:33)

Be careful for nothing; but in everything by prayer and supplication with thanksgiving let your requests be made known unto God. (Philippians 4:6)

Thou wilt keep him in perfect peace, whose mind is stayed on thee: because he trusteth in thee. (Isaiah 26:3)

Casting all your care upon him; for he careth for you. (1 Peter 5:7)

I will both lay me down in peace, and sleep: for thou, LORD, only makest me dwell in safety. (Psalms 4:8)

When thou liest down, thou shalt not be afraid: yea, thou shalt lie down, and thy sleep shall be sweet. (Proverbs 3:24)

Now the God of hope fill you with all joy and peace in believing, that ye may abound in hope, through the power of the Holy Ghost. (Romans 15:13)

SISTERHOOD *a* VILLAGE

Thoughts to Ponder

One of the greatest feelings in the world is to have a sisterhood that is genuine and true. It's a beautiful thing when sisters cause you to leap over mountains because they believe in you. Your ideas and dreams become theirs. You conquer all things as a team. Together, life is sweeter, empowering and easier. When you are broken, sisterhood serves as a shelter when it's raining and promotes joy when the sun is shining on your life. A gift that every woman should desire to have is a sisterhood.

The Challenge

1. **What are some challenges you have faced or have witnessed that create conflict among women? Explain.**

   _____
   _____
   _____

2. **Do you believe sisterhood is necessary? Why or why not?**

   _____
   _____
   _____

3. **Give an example of sisterhood that has helped to catapult you?**

   _____
   _____
   _____

4. **How do you deal with friends with different personalities which can be at times challenging within your sisterhood?**

   _____
   _____
   _____

5. **What advice would you give to a woman that struggles with holding onto meaningful relationships?**

   _____
   _____
   _____

6. How would you handle disagreements within your own sisterhood?

_____

_____

_____

_____

_____

7. Write your own story using this prompt: Sisterhood is rewarding

_____

_____

_____

_____

_____

Kingdom Words

Write three kingdom words that will empower you to be better, victorious and triumphant in relation to this proverb.

1. _____

2. _____

3. _____

Checkpoints

Be kindly affectioned one to another with brotherly love; in honour preferring one another. (Romans 12:10)

Two are better than one; because they have a good reward for their labour. For if they fall, the one will lift up his fellow: but woe to him that is alone when he falleth; for he hath not another to help him up. Again, if two lie together, then they have heat: but how can one be warm alone? (Ecclesiastes 4:9-11)

Confess your faults one to another, and pray one for another, that ye may be healed. The effectual fervent prayer of a righteous man availeth much. (James 5:16)

If it be possible, as much as lieth in you, live peaceably with all men. (Romans 12:18)

Greater love hath no man than this, that a man lay down his life for his friends. (John 15:13)

A friend loveth at all times, and a brother is born for adversity. (Proverbs 17:17)

Ye have heard that it hath been said, Thou shalt love thy neighbour, and hate thine enemy. But I say unto you, Love your enemies, bless them that curse you, do good to them that hate you, and pray for them which despitefully use you, and persecute you; That ye may be the children of your Father which is in heaven: for he maketh his sun to rise on the evil and on the good, and sendeth rain on the just and on the unjust. (Matthew 5:43-45)

PROVERB ELEVEN
A CONSTANT FRIEND

Thoughts to Ponder

She is constant. You never need to question her stance for she remains true, at all times. When you cry, she cries with you. She helps you to carry what is too heavy for you to bear. When there is war, she is your warrior. You never have to stand alone for she has your back. She loves you at all times. Her friendship never fades away. She pays attention to your stare and knows when you are hurting. She takes note of the tone of your voice and addresses you with concern. She is assigned to your life. She is your Naomi.

The Challenge

1. These days, are constant friends hard to find?

_____

_____

_____

_____

2. Are good friendships hard to cultivate? Explain the reasons why and explore ways you can be part of the solution.

_____

_____

_____

_____

3. Were there times when you knew you were not a good friend? If so, what did you do to change or to be a better friend?

_____

_____

_____

_____

4. Have you been honest and transparent with your friend(s) when you have been hurt and have held a grudge? Explain the effects of honesty.

_____

_____

_____

_____

5. What are the qualities of a great friend?

_____

_____

_____

Key Thoughts

6. How do you truly value friendship?

_____

_____

_____

7. Write your own story using this prompt: A friend is supportive and also

_____

_____

_____

Kingdom Words

Write three kingdom words that will empower you to be better, victorious and triumphant in relation to this proverb.

1. _____

2. _____

3. _____

Checkpoints

And the Scripture was fulfilled that says, "Abraham believed God, and it was counted to him as righteousness" – and he was called a friend of God. (James 2:23 ESV)

No longer do I call you servants, for the servant does not know what his master is doing; but I have called you friends, for all that I have heard from my Father I have made known to you. (John 15:15 ESV)

Greater love has no one than this, that someone lay down his life for his friends. (John 15:13 ESV)

A man of many companions may come to ruin, but there is a friend who sticks closer than a brother. (Proverbs 18:24 ESV)

A dishonest man spreads strife, and a whisperer separates close friends. (Proverbs 16:28 ESV)

Open rebuke is better than love carefully concealed. Faithful are the wounds of a friend, but the kisses of an enemy are deceitful. (Proverbs 27:5-6 NJKV)

Do not be deceived: "Bad company ruins good morals." (1 Corinthians 15:33 ESV)

Two are better than one, because they have a good reward for their toil. For if they fall, one will lift up his fellow. But woe to him who is alone when he falls and has not another to lift him up! Again, if two lie together, they keep warm, but how can one keep warm alone? And though a man might prevail against one who is alone, two will withstand him—a threefold cord is not quickly broken. (Ecclesiastes 4:9-12 ESV)

PROVERB TWELVE

LAUGH *in his* FACE

Thoughts to Ponder

Learning to laugh takes practice but you can choose to laugh. God will give you strength to overcome the areas that the enemy strategically designed to prohibit you from laughing. God will make a way of escape from the paradigms that the enemy has set up for you. It's time for you to laugh in his face.

The Challenge

1. What experiences from your past has the enemy tried to hold you in bondage to? How long have you faced this plot?

_____
_____
_____
_____
_____

2. Find a scripture that relates to the bondage you identified and write a confession. Read your confession out loud, each day, and learn to laugh.

_____
_____
_____
_____
_____

3. Identify a time in your life when you chose to laugh rather than cry.

_____
_____
_____
_____
_____

4. Why do people mask their hurt rather than expose their truth and be healed?

_____
_____
_____
_____

Key Thoughts

5. **Explain the scripture, Proverbs 17:22: "A joyful heart is good medicine."**

_____
_____
_____
_____
_____
_____

6. **Write your own story using this prompt: I will laugh and soar over**

_____
_____
_____
_____
_____
_____
_____
_____

Kingdom Words

Write three kingdom words that will empower you to be better, victorious and triumphant in relation to this proverb.

1. _____

2. _____

3. _____

Checkpoints

Rejoice evermore. Pray without ceasing. In everything give thanks: for this is the will of God in Christ Jesus concerning you. (1 Thessalonians 5:16-18)

Thou wilt shew me the path of life: in thy presence is fulness of joy; at thy right hand there are pleasures for evermore. (Psalms 16:11)

Happy is the man that findeth wisdom, and the man that getteth understanding. (Proverbs 3:13)

A joyful heart is good medicine, But a broken spirit dries up the bones. (Proverbs 17:22 NASB)

Why art thou cast down, O my soul? and why art thou disquieted within me? hope thou in God: for I shall yet praise him, who is the health of my countenance, and my God. (Psalms 42:11)

Then our mouth was filled with laughter, And our tongue with singing. Then they said among the nations, "The Lord has done great things for them." (Psalms 126:2 NJKV)

Blessed are ye that hunger now: for ye shall be filled. Blessed are ye that weep now: for ye shall laugh. (Luke 6:21)

Till he fill thy mouth with laughing, and thy lips with rejoicing. (Job 8:21)

25

BEAUTY, BRAINS *and* FAVOR

Thoughts to Ponder

Royalty, beauty, flawlessness, intelligence, and brilliance is all wrapped in who God created you to be. You were created to do great exploits in the earth. God has favored you to be a queen over all that you set your mind to do. You are royal, and you need no one's opinion to simply be you. Shine bright and own your stance on the earth. Be bold for God has given you favor.

The Challenge

1. Is there a task God has given you that you have not yet completed? If so, write it down. Evaluate the reason behind your disobedience or delay.

_____
_____
_____
_____

2. Write a declaration that will help you complete what God has instructed you to do.

_____
_____
_____
_____

3. Read and dissect 1 Peter 2:9: "But ye *are* a chosen generation, a royal priesthood, an holy nation, a peculiar people; that ye should shew forth the praises of him who hath called you out of darkness into his marvellous light."

_____
_____
_____
_____

4. Esther was used to save an entire nation. How will you stand in the gap and intercede for your family?

_____
_____
_____
_____

Key Thoughts

5. **Explain why favor is more valuable than money?**

_____
_____
_____
_____

6. **Write your own story using this prompt: God has favored me to be**

_____
_____
_____
_____

Kingdom Words

Write three kingdom words that will empower you to be better, victorious and triumphant in relation to this proverb.

1. _____
2. _____
3. _____

Checkpoints

And Jesus increased in wisdom and in stature and in favor with God and man. May this be our portion, May we continually increase in wisdom and in spiritual stature, pleasing God in all we do, and finding favor with both God and man. Amen. (Luke 2:52 ESV)

May the favor of the Lord our God rest on us; establish the work of our hands for us – yes, establish the work of our hands. (Psalms 90:17 NIV)

For you bless the righteous, O Lord; you cover him with favor as with a shield. (Psalms 5:12 ESV)

And the Lord said to Moses, "This very thing that you have spoken I will do, for you have found favor in my sight, and I know you by name." (Exodus 33:17 ESV)

When the turn came for Esther the daughter of Abihail the uncle of Mordecai, who had taken her as his own daughter, to go in to the king, she asked for nothing except what Hegai the king's eunuch, who had charge of the women, advised. Now Esther was winning favor in the eyes of all who saw her. (Esther 2:15-16 ESV)

From his abundance we have all received one gracious blessing after another. (John 1:16 NLT)

But let it be the hidden man of the heart, in that which is not corruptible, even the ornament of a meek and quiet spirit, which is in the sight of God of great price. (1 Peter 3:4)

If any of you lacks wisdom, let him ask of God, who gives to all liberally and without reproach, and it will be given to him. (James 1:5 NKJV)

Wisdom is the principal thing; therefore get wisdom. And in all your getting, get understanding. (Proverbs 4:7)

IT'S *as* CRUEL *as* ~the~ GRAVE – JEALOUSY

Thoughts to Ponder

Jealously! Decree and declare that you are not a jealous woman. Jealousy is not the posture of your heart. You are free for God has rid you of this strong, cold and detrimental emotion that would eventually cause your life to be empty. See yourself better.

The Challenge

1. How has jealousy manifested in your life? Explain.

_____

_____

_____

_____

_____

2. Have you ever been jealous? If so, how did you overcome this spirit?

_____

_____

_____

_____

_____

3. What advice can you give someone who is excessively jealous and cause them to see that jealousy is a destructive emotion?

_____

_____

_____

_____

4. How does jealousy affect a person's behavior?

_____

_____

_____

_____

Key Thoughts

5. **Define the difference between being envious and being jealous.**

_____

_____

_____

_____

_____

6. **Write your own story using this prompt: The spirit of jealousy can be**

_____

_____

_____

_____

_____

Kingdom Words

Write three kingdom words that will empower you to be better, victorious and triumphant in relation to this proverb.

1. _____

2. _____

3. _____

Checkpoints

But the fruit of the Spirit is love, joy, peace, patience, kindness, goodness, faithfulness. (Galatians 5:22 ESV)

For where jealousy and selfish ambition exist, there will be disorder and every vile practice. (James 3:16 ESV)

You desire and do not have, so you murder. You covet and cannot obtain, so you fight and quarrel. You do not have, because you do not ask. You ask and do not receive, because you ask wrongly, to spend it on your passions. (James 4:2-3 ESV)

A tranquil heart gives life to the flesh, but envy makes the bones rot. (Proverbs 14:30 ESV)

No temptation has overtaken you that is not common to man. God is faithful, and he will not let you be tempted beyond your ability, but with the temptation he will also provide the way of escape, that you may be able to endure it. (1 Corinthians 10:13 ESV)

Now the works of the flesh are evident: sexual immorality, impurity, sensuality, idolatry, sorcery, enmity, strife, jealousy, fits of anger, rivalries, dissensions, divisions, envy, drunkenness, orgies, and things like these. I warn you, as I warned you before, that those who do such things will not inherit the kingdom of God. (Galatians 5:19-21 ESV)

Anyone who does not love does not know God, because God is love. (1 John 4:8 ESV)

Set me as a seal upon your heart, As a seal upon your arm; For love is as strong as death, Jealousy as cruel as the grave; Its flames are flames of fire, A most vehement flame. (Song of Solomon 8:6 NKJV)

Let nothing be done through strife or vainglory; but in lowliness of mind let each esteem other better than themselves. (Philippians 2:3)

THE CATALYST *of* PRIDE IS I

Thoughts to Ponder

God promises us a life of wholeness. Proud is not who you are. Pride will not dominate your heart for your heart is filled with humility. Humility warms your soul and invites the Holy Spirit to dwell. Rid yourself of the ugly look of haughtiness by prayer and fasting. There is a life of victory springing up for you walk in humility.

The Challenge

1. Think on 1 Peter 3:4: "Rather, it should be that of your inner self, the unfading beauty of a gentle and quiet spirit, which is of great worth in God's sight. (NIV)" When people see you, do they see pride? Do they see the unfading beauty of a gentle spirit?

_____

_____

_____

2. Explain 1 Peter 3:4 in your own words:

_____

_____

_____

3. Has pride hindered your walk with God? How has pride subtracted from your life?

_____

_____

_____

4. It is stated in Proverbs 16:18, "Pride goeth before destruction, and an haughty spirit before a fall." Explain this passage of scripture.

_____

_____

_____

5. Is there such a thing as good pride and bad pride? Explain.

_____

_____

_____

6. **Why is pride defined as a feeling of deep pleasure and self-gratification?**

_____

_____

_____

_____

_____

_____

7. **Write your own story using this prompt: Pride is a strong spirit and I choose**

_____

_____

_____

_____

_____

_____

_____

Kingdom Words

Write three kingdom words that will empower you to be better, victorious and triumphant in relation to this proverb.

1. _____

2. _____

3. _____

Checkpoints

When pride cometh, then cometh shame: but with the lowly is wisdom. (Proverbs 11:2)

Every one that is proud in heart is an abomination to the LORD: though hand join in hand, he shall not be unpunished. (Proverbs 16:5)

A man's pride shall bring him low: but honour shall uphold the humble in spirit. (Proverbs 29:23)

Pride goeth before destruction, and an haughty spirit before a fall. (Proverbs 16:18)

For if a man think himself to be something, when he is nothing, he deceiveth himself. (Galatians 6:3)

But he giveth more grace. Wherefore he saith, God resisteth the proud, but giveth grace unto the humble. (James 4:6)

Let another man praise thee, and not thine own mouth; a stranger, and not thine own lips. (Proverbs 27:2)

Seest thou a man wise in his own conceit? there is more hope of a fool than of him. (Proverbs 26:12)

MY KINGDOM MAN

Thoughts to Ponder

The man you prayed for, God shall grant your request. Don't lose sight of the precious prayer you have faithfully prayed. Although you may get weary in your waiting, remember that our great God is faithful. While waiting, celebrate and serve God, and He will speak volumes of love to your soul. That kingdom man shall be your treasure chest. Just believe your kingdom man is coming in Gods timing. So, be ready.

The Challenge

1. What are the obstacles you face in submitting to your husband?

_____

_____

_____

2. What areas of your life can you change to help your relationship?

_____

_____

_____

3. What is an area that you desire your Kingdom man to do better in and how can you communicate this desire to him?

_____

_____

_____

4. Make a list of your marriage goals. When you are ready, share these marriage goals with your husband.

_____

_____

_____

5. If you are married, describe this statement: "Marriage takes work."

_____

_____

_____

_____

6. Do you struggle with speaking the words, "I love you" to your husband? If so, explain.

_____

_____

_____

Key Thoughts

7. What is the one special attribute you pray for in a kingdom man and why?

_____

_____

_____

8. Write your own story using this prompt: I have waited for my kingdom man and finally

_____

_____

_____

Kingdom Words

Write three kingdom words that will empower you to be better, victorious and triumphant in relation to this proverb.

1. _____

2. _____

3. _____

Checkpoints

In all things shewing thyself a pattern of good works: in doctrine shewing uncorruptness, gravity, sincerity. (Titus 2:7)

When I was a child, I spake as a child, I understood as a child, I thought as a child: but when I became a man, I put away childish things. (1 Corinthians 13:11)

But if any provide not for his own, and especially for those of his own house, he hath denied the faith, and is worse than an infidel. (1 Timothy 5:8)

Praise ye the LORD. Blessed is the man that feareth the LORD, that delighteth greatly in his commandments. His seed shall be mighty upon earth: the generation of the upright shall be blessed. Wealth and riches shall be in his house: and his righteousness endureth for ever. Unto the upright there ariseth light in the darkness: [he is] gracious, and full of compassion, and righteous. A good man sheweth favour, and lendeth: he will guide his affairs with discretion. Surely he shall not be moved for ever: the righteous shall be in everlasting remembrance. He shall not be afraid of evil tidings: his heart is fixed, trusting in the LORD. (Psalms 112:1-7)

The steps of a good man are ordered by the LORD: and he delighteth in his way. (Psalms 37:23)

Seest thou a man diligent in his business? he shall stand before kings; he shall not stand before mean men. (Proverbs 22:29)

For the husband is the head of the wife, even as Christ is the head of the church: and he is the saviour of the body. Therefore as the church is subject unto Christ, so let the wives be to their own husbands in everything. Husbands, love your wives, even as Christ also loved the church, and gave himself for it. (Ephesians 5:23-25)

THAT OTHER KIND *of* MAN

Thoughts to Ponder

Can you remember thinking, "If I could just get over this *other* kind of man?" You know those bad boys. Well, you *can* overcome and heal, by faith. You deserve the very best in your life. You don't deserve a fairy tale wrapped in a big lie. You shall have God's best. God knows when you are ready. Wait and you will have your divine love with a white picket fence. Dreams do come true.

The Challenge

1. Write down what you earnestly need God to do in your life during your seven-day consecration.

   _____
   _____
   _____

2. Pray and meditate on the Word. Empty yourself before God and thank Him, in advance, for strength to wait for your kingdom man. What are some things you can work on while you wait?

   _____
   _____
   _____

3. When did you recognize that you were in a relationship with a con man and how did you deal with this reality?

   _____
   _____
   _____

4. How can you keep your flesh under subjection and remain sexually dormant when dating?

   _____
   _____
   _____

5. Did you have to recover from low self-esteem due to years of being stuck in a painful dating experience?

   _____
   _____
   _____
   _____

6. Do you feel that you are worthy of the kingdom man that God has promised you?

_____

_____

_____

_____

Key Thoughts

7. What Godly advice do you give to a friend that is in an abusive relationship?

_____

_____

_____

8. Write your own story using this prompt: I pray for the strength to

_____

_____

_____

Kingdom Words

Write three kingdom words that will empower you to be better, victorious and triumphant in relation to this proverb.

1. _____

2. _____

3. _____

Checkpoints

I can do all things through Christ which strengtheneth me. (Philippians 4:13)

Devote yourselves to prayer with an alert mind and a thankful heart. (Colossians 4:2 NLT)

Watch ye, stand fast in the faith, quit you like men, be strong. (1 Corinthians 16:13)

Keep alert at all times. And pray that you might be strong enough to escape these coming horrors and stand before the Son of Man. (Luke 21:36 NLT)

But seek ye first the kingdom of God, and his righteousness; and all these things shall be added unto you. (Matthew 6:33)

Marriage should be honored by all, and the marriage bed kept pure, for God will judge the adulterer and all the sexually immoral. (Hebrews 13:4 NIV)

No temptation has overtaken you except what is common to mankind. And God is faithful; he will not let you be tempted beyond what you can bear. But when you are tempted, he will also provide a way out so that you can endure it. (1 Corinthians 10:13 NIV)

As the deer pants for streams of water, so my soul pants for you, my God. (Psalms 42:1 NIV)

SAFE, SECURE, *and* SETTLED

Thoughts to Ponder

Our children are the greatest gift that God gave us; so we cherish and handle them with care. The responsibility for care and love is an honor from God. How do/will you handle the seed God gave you? Parents have a great investment to make in the lives of their children. Our children never outgrow our love. Remember that.

The Challenge

1. **What challenges have you faced in raising your children?**

_____

_____

_____

_____

2. **How have you used such challenges to impact their lives positively?**

_____

_____

_____

_____

3. **Take a moment to reflect. How have you invested in the lives of your children?**

_____

_____

_____

_____

4. **Do you speak empowering words such as, "I love you" or "I'm proud of you"? If not, why?**

_____

_____

_____

5. **Explain the difference between being a parent and being a counselor?**

_____

_____

_____

6. Do family dynamics play a major role in the development of a child? Explain.

_____
_____
_____
_____

7. How can you be a better parent? Explain in detail.

_____
_____
_____
_____

8. Write your own story using this prompt: I praise God that my children are

_____
_____
_____
_____

Kingdom Words

Write three kingdom words that will empower you to be better, victorious and triumphant in relation to this proverb.

1. _____

2. _____

3. _____

Checkpoints

Train up a child in the way he should go: and when he is old, he will not depart from it. (Proverbs 22:6)

And, ye fathers, provoke not your children to wrath: but bring them up in the nurture and admonition of the Lord. (Ephesians 6:4)

And all thy children shall be taught of the LORD; and great [shall be] the peace of thy children. (Isaiah 54:13)

A good man leaveth an inheritance to his children's children: and the wealth of the sinner is laid up for the just. (Proverbs 13:22)

Let no man despise thy youth; but be thou an example of the believers, in word, in conversation, in charity, in spirit, in faith, in purity. (1 Timothy 4:12)

My son, keep thy father's commandment, and forsake not the law of thy mother: Bind them continually upon thine heart, and tie them about thy neck. When thou goest, it shall lead thee; when thou sleepest, it shall keep thee; and when thou awakest, it shall talk with thee. (Proverbs 6:20:22)

And he took a child, and set him in the midst of them: and when he had taken him in his arms, he said unto them, Whosoever shall receive one of such children in my name, receiveth me: and whosoever shall receive me, receiveth not me, but him that sent me. (Mark 9:36-37)

Take heed that ye despise not one of these little ones; for I say unto you, That in heaven their angels do always behold the face of my Father which is in heaven. (Matthew 18:10)

YOU SEE MY FLAWS, BUT GOD SEES DIFFERENTLY

Thoughts to Ponder

Are you glad that God sees your heart and your flaws? God will adjust as He sees fit to do so. We are to love. Period. Let us offer love with a welcoming attitude rather than judgment. One thing about life, we will all encounter a judgmental person; nevertheless, be thankful that God has the antidote for our flaws, love.

The Challenge

1. How can you help those who have been wounded because they did not feel good enough?

_____

_____

_____

2. How do you witness/minister to someone who has been wounded at church?

_____

_____

_____

3. How can you make an individual understand that God loves them, and He sees them differently?

_____

_____

_____

4. How can believers refrain from being judgmental?

_____

_____

_____

5. How can you demonstrate kindness by giving a gift of love to a new believer and present it to them when God leads you to do so.

_____

_____

_____

Key Thoughts

6. **What advice would you give to a new believer that would encourage them to stay focused on God?**

_____

_____

_____

_____

7. **Write your own story using this prompt: I may be flawed, but my faithful God has**

_____

_____

_____

_____

Kingdom Words

Write three kingdom words that will empower you to be better, victorious and triumphant in relation to this proverb.

1. _____
2. _____
3. _____

Checkpoints

Therefore if any man be in Christ, he is a new creature: old things are passed away; behold, all things are become new. (2 Corinthians 5:17)

Blessed be the God and Father of our Lord Jesus Christ, who according to His great mercy has caused us to be born again to a living hope through the resurrection of Jesus Christ from the dead. (1 Peter 1:3)

For you are all sons of God through faith in Christ Jesus. (Galatians 3:6)

But what saith it? The word is nigh thee, even in thy mouth, and in thy heart: that is, the word of faith, which we preach; that if you confess with your mouth Jesus as Lord, and believe in your heart that God raised Him from the dead, you will be saved; for with the heart a person believes, resulting in righteousness, and with the mouth he confesses, resulting in salvation. (Romans 10:8-10)

For God so loved the world, that He gave His only begotten Son, that whoever believes in Him shall not perish, but have eternal life." For God sent not his Son into the world to condemn the world; but that the world through him might be saved. He that believeth on him is not condemned: but he that believeth not is condemned already, because he hath not believed in the name of the only begotten Son of God. (John 3:16-18)

But God commendeth his own love toward us, in that, while we were yet sinners, Christ died for us. (Romans 5:8 ASV)

Judge not, that ye be not judged. For with what judgment ye judge, ye shall be judged: and with what measure ye mete, it shall be measured to you again. And why beholdest thou the mote that is in thy brother's eye, but considerest not the beam that is in thine own eye? (Matthew 7:1-3)

I AM GREATER *than* FEAR

Thoughts to Ponder

Finally, you have surmounted the very thing in your past that crippled you, fear. You discovered, through prayer, that you are greater than that which desired to hold you captive. You will no longer be a hostage to the feeling that has no face. Fear is one deadly design of the enemy but through God, you are stronger, and you trump fear. Declare, today, that you shall not visit the enemy called fear.

The Challenge

1. **Pray and ask God to reveal to you what causes you to walk in the spirit of fear.**

_____
_____
_____
_____
_____

2. **Write a personal confession that applies to the truth God revealed to you and apply scripture to your confession.**

_____
_____
_____
_____
_____

3. **Finish this statement: Fear has no face, but I fear**

_____
_____
_____
_____
_____

4. **Do you believe that our fears are self-created? Explain.**

_____
_____
_____
_____

5. How have you allowed fear to cripple you and keep you in a holding pattern?

_____

_____

_____

_____

_____

6. Write your own story using this prompt: I will not allow the spirit of fear to

_____

_____

_____

_____

_____

Kingdom Words

Write three kingdom words that will empower you to be better, victorious and triumphant in relation to this proverb.

1. _____

2. _____

3. _____

Checkpoints

Fear thou not; for I am with thee: be not dismayed; for I [am] thy God: I will strengthen thee; yea, I will help thee; yea, I will uphold thee with the right hand of my righteousness. (Isaiah 41:10)

For God hath not given us the spirit of fear; but of power, and of love, and of a sound mind. (2 Timothy 1:7)

There is no fear in love; but perfect love casteth out fear: because fear hath torment. He that feareth is not made perfect in love. (1 John 4:18)

For ye have not received the spirit of bondage again to fear; but ye have received the Spirit of adoption, whereby we cry, Abba, Father. (Romans 8:15)

But now thus saith the LORD that created thee, O Jacob, and he that formed thee, O Israel, Fear not: for I have redeemed thee, I have called thee by thy name; thou art mine. When thou passest through the waters, I will be with thee; and through the rivers, they shall not overflow thee: when thou walkest through the fire, thou shalt not be burned; neither shall the flame kindle upon thee. (Isaiah 43:1-2)

Fear thou not; for I [am] with thee: be not dismayed; for I [am] thy God: I will strengthen thee; yea, I will help thee; yea, I will uphold thee with the right hand of my righteousness. (Isaiah 41:10)

For I am persuaded, that neither death, nor life, nor angels, nor principalities, nor powers, nor things present, nor things to come, Nor height, nor depth, nor any other creature, shall be able to separate us from the love of God, which is in Christ Jesus our Lord. (Romans 8:38-39)

NEVER ~too~ LATE ~to~ BE FREE

Thoughts to Ponder

It's a sweet feeling to be free. Just for a moment, reflect on the feeling of bondage which was incredibly unhealthy. It was designed to keep you from being who God created you to be. Now that you are free, stay free and don't return to your holding patterns of yesterday. God desires for you to live. God desires that your mind stay renewed and fresh.

The Challenge

1. Seek the Lord, through prayer, and ask God to help you identify what has kept you from moving forward in life. Be honest with yourself.

   _____
   _____
   _____

2. What is the freedom that the Word speaks of?

   _____
   _____
   _____

3. Were there times in your life when you felt you were free but it was only a false feeling? Give an example.

   _____
   _____
   _____

4. Freedom means many things to many people. What does freedom mean to you?

   _____
   _____
   _____

5. Describe an emotional, physical, and/or psychological infirmity that kept you bent over for years? What was so painful that you almost did not recover from?

   _____
   _____
   _____

Key Thoughts

6. Freedom is your promise from God, so how will you maintain your freedom? Ask the Holy Spirit to lead you to a scripture that will help you in this quest to remain free.

_____
_____
_____
_____
_____

7. Write your own story using this prompt: I am free from

_____
_____
_____
_____
_____

Kingdom Words

Write three kingdom words that will empower you to be better, victorious and triumphant in relation to this proverb.

1. _____
2. _____
3. _____

Checkpoints

Therefore there is now no condemnation for those who are in Christ Jesus. For the law of the Spirit of life in Christ Jesus has set you free from the law of sin and of death. (Romans 8:1-2)

That the creation itself will be set free from its bondage to corruption and obtain the freedom of the glory of the children of God. (Romans 8:21 ESV)

Now the Lord is the Spirit, and where the Spirit of the Lord is, there is freedom. (2 Corinthians 3:17 ESV)

For freedom Christ has set us free; stand firm therefore, and do not submit again to a yoke of slavery. (Galatians 5:1 ESV)

If the Son therefore shall make you free, ye shall be free indeed. (John 8:36)

For the law of the Spirit of life in Christ Jesus hath made me free from the law of sin and death. (Romans 8:2)

Stand fast therefore in the liberty wherewith Christ hath made us free, and be not entangled again with the yoke of bondage. (Galatians 5:1)

For by grace are ye saved through faith; and that not of yourselves: it is the gift of God. (Ephesians 2:8)

TO HONOR HER IS *the* GREATEST JOY

Thoughts to Ponder

Consider this: You are here for she was here, first. A mother is a joy and a benefit to your life. She makes life easier for her wisdom is life. Her love is heavenly. She pushes you past your insecurities and demonstrates to you what integrity looks like. She mirrors the attributes of God. She teaches you to take a deep breath and ride the waves of life and reminds you that problems are only in our pasture for a season. She is your source of spiritual and emotional support. There's truly nothing like a mother's love.

The Challenge

1. Take time out to make your mother feel special. Take her to dinner, a movie, set up a picnic, or go for a walk and let her know how valuable she has been in your life. What are some other ideas?

   _____
   _____
   _____

2. Write down reasons why you are successful because of your mother.

   _____
   _____
   _____

3. What does it mean to honor your mother according to Exodus 20:12?

   _____
   _____
   _____

4. Children tend to take their mothers for granted, unknowingly. Give examples.

   _____
   _____
   _____

5. What attribute do you strive to have that your mother possessed?

   _____
   _____
   _____

Key Thoughts

6. **What is a question you would like to ask your mother and why haven't you asked her?**

_____

_____

_____

_____

_____

7. **Write your own story using this prompt: Being a mother has been the most**

_____

_____

_____

_____

_____

Kingdom Words

Write three kingdom words that will empower you to be better, victorious and triumphant in relation to this proverb.

1. _____

2. _____

3. _____

Checkpoints

The rod and reproof give wisdom: but a child left to himself bringeth his mother to shame. (Proverbs 29:15)

Give respect to your father and mother, for without them you wouldn't be here. And don't neglect them when they grow old. Embrace the truth and hold it close. Don't let go of wisdom, instruction and life-giving understanding. When a father observes his child living in godliness, he is ecstatic with joy-nothing makes him prouder! So may your father's heart bust with joy and your mother's soul be filled with gladness because of you. (Proverbs 23:22-25 TPT)

You formed my innermost being, shaping my delicate inside and my intricate outside, and you wove them all together in my mother's womb. (Psalms 139:13)

Who can find a virtuous woman? for her price is far above rubies. (Proverbs 31:10)

She openeth her mouth with wisdom; and in her tongue is the law of kindness. She looketh well to the ways of her household, and eateth not the bread of idleness. (Proverbs 31:26-27)

But speak thou the things which become sound doctrine: That the aged men be sober, grave, temperate, sound in faith, in charity, in patience. The aged women likewise, that they be in behaviour as becometh holiness, not false accusers, not given to much wine, teachers of good things; That they may teach the young women to be sober, to love their husbands, to love their children, To be discreet, chaste, keepers at home, good, obedient to their own husbands, that the word of God be not blasphemed. (Titus 2:1-5)

Honour thy father and thy mother: that thy days may be long upon the land which the Lord thy God giveth thee. (Exodus 20:12)

Children, obey your parents in all things: for this is well pleasing unto the Lord. (Colossians 3:20)

THE ABSOLUTE TRUTH

Thoughts to Ponder

It's calming and brings peace. While in the midst of brokenness, it heals and shields you from the wiles of the enemy. It is the truth. It is life. It is empowering. It is our strength. It is the Word of God. We hide it in our heart for it is God speaking to us. The Word is our absolute truth in all matters.

The Challenge

1. **How often do you read and study the Word of God?**

   _____

   _____

   _____

   _____

   _____

2. **What distractions do you face while reading the Word, and how could you defeat these distractions?**

   _____

   _____

   _____

   _____

   _____

3. **Explain this statement, the Word of God is the absolute truth is all matters.**

   _____

   _____

   _____

   _____

   _____

4. **How has the Word helped you to maintain stability in your life? Explain.**

   _____

   _____

   _____

   _____

Key Thoughts

5. How would you introduce God's Word to a new believer and what scriptures would you give them to help them develop a relationship with Christ?

_____
_____
_____
_____
_____

6. Write your own story using this prompt: The Word of God is

_____
_____
_____
_____
_____

Kingdom Words

Write three kingdom words that will empower you to be better, victorious and triumphant in relation to this proverb.

1. _____
2. _____
3. _____

Checkpoints

For the word of God is quick, and powerful, and sharper than any twoedged sword, piercing even to the dividing asunder of soul and spirit, and of the joints and marrow, and is a discerner of the thoughts and intents of the heart. (Hebrews 4:12)

But he answered and said, It is written, Man shall not live by bread alone, but by every word that proceedeth out of the mouth of God. (Matthew 4:4)

Heaven and earth will pass away, but my words will never pass away. (Matthew 24:35 NIV)

Sanctify them through thy truth: thy word is truth. (John 17:17)

It is the spirit that quickeneth; the flesh profiteth nothing: the words that I speak unto you, they are spirit, and they are life. (John 6:63)

All scripture is given by inspiration of God, and is profitable for doctrine, for reproof, for correction, for instruction in righteousness: "That the man of God may be perfect, throughly furnished unto all good works." (2 Timothy 3:16)

Thy word have I hid in mine heart, that I might not sin against thee. (Psalms 119:11)

Your word is a lamp for my feet, a light on my path. (Psalms 119:105 NIV)

SILENCE

Thoughts to Ponder

Speak that which is in your heart to speak. Your voice is powerful and the energy of your mouth holds vibration. Vibrations from your voice will cause things to shift and move when you speak with truth and wisdom. Silence can be a trick making one feel that if they speak confusion will be birthed. No, lives shall be changed. Don't remain silent. Use your voice as a tool of change. Please, speak up!

The Challenge

1. In prayer, write down barriers that have caused you to keep silent in the past.

_____

_____

_____

2. Do you need help from God to break the silence about a current situation in your life? Would speaking into that situation bring deliverance to your life or others? Be honest with yourself. Ask God to help you voice your feelings with wisdom and not be silent.

_____

_____

_____

3. Has silence been a stronghold in your life due to fear? Explain.

_____

_____

_____

4. How do you overcome the fear of confrontation and express your heartfelt concerns?

_____

_____

_____

5. Are you considered a pushover for not speaking up or do you consider yourself a peacemaker?

_____

_____

_____

Key Thoughts

6. Is silence just the absence of noise or does it mean more than that? Explain.

_____

_____

_____

_____

_____

7. Write your own story using this prompt: I will no longer remain in silence and allow

_____

_____

_____

_____

_____

Kingdom Words

Write three kingdom words that will empower you to be better, victorious and triumphant in relation to this proverb.

1. _____

2. _____

3. _____

Checkpoints

A soft answer turns away wrath, but a harsh word stirs up anger. (Proverbs 15:1 ESV)

I tell you, on the day of judgment people will give account for every careless word they speak. (Matthew 12:36 ESV)

Let your speech always be gracious, seasoned with salt, so that you may know how you ought to answer each person. (Colossians 4:6 ESV)

Let the words of my mouth and the meditation of my heart be acceptable in your sight, O LORD, my rock and my redeemer. (Psalms 19:14 ESV)

The mouth of the righteous utters wisdom, and his tongue speaks justice. (Psalms 37:30 ESV)

Anxiety in a man's heart weighs him down, but a good word makes him glad. (Proverb 12:25 ESV)

Let no corrupting talk come out of your mouths, but only such as is good for building up, as fits the occasion, that it may give grace to those who hear. (Ephesians 4:29 ESV)

Finally, brethren, whatsoever things are true, whatsoever things are honest, whatsoever things are just, whatsoever things are pure, whatsoever things are lovely, whatsoever things are of good report; if there be any virtue, and if there be any praise, think on these things. (Philippians 4:8)

GIVERS *and* TAKERS

Thoughts to Ponder

You shall be a blessing in the earth for God's glory. Freely, you shall give as a demonstration of who God is. As you release your gifts to others, God will, in turn, bless you. Taking is not a part of who you are for continually taking has no return. Declare that you will be an instrument of goodness in the earth.

The Challenge

1. I challenge you to give the very thing God has been asking you to give.

   _____
   _____
   _____
   _____

2. Be honest with yourself. What barriers caused you to be disobedient to God? Write the barriers down and promise yourself that these barriers won't occur again.

   _____
   _____
   _____
   _____

3. Write a confession declaring that you will be a blessing for the Kingdom. Revisit it daily.

   _____
   _____
   _____
   _____

4. Describe emotional takers in relationships?

   _____
   _____
   _____

5. Do you feel that taking is a learned behavior? Please explain.

   _____
   _____
   _____

6. Describe your truth about givers vs. takers.

_____
_____
_____
_____
_____
_____
_____

7. Write your own story using this prompt: I have learned that taking

_____
_____
_____
_____
_____
_____
_____

Kingdom Words

Write three kingdom words that will empower you to be better, victorious and triumphant in relation to this proverb.

1. _____
2. _____
3. _____

Checkpoints

Give, and it shall be given unto you; good measure, pressed down, and shaken together, and running over, shall men give into your bosom. For with the same measure that ye mete withal it shall be measured to you again. (Luke 6:38)

Every good gift and every perfect gift is from above, and cometh down from the Father of lights, with whom is no variableness, neither shadow of turning. (James 1:17)

Be hospitable to one another without grumbling. (1 Peter 1:4)

But my God shall supply all your need according to his riches in glory by Christ Jesus. (Philippians 4:19)

But this I say, He which soweth sparingly shall reap also sparingly; and he which soweth bountifully shall reap also bountifully. Every man according as he purposeth in his heart, so let him give; not grudgingly, or of necessity: for God loveth a cheerful giver. (2 Corinthians 9:6-7)

A gift opens the way and ushers the giver into the presence of the great. (Proverbs 18:16 NIV)

For if the willingness is there, the gift is acceptable according to what one has, not according to what one does not have. (2 Corinthians 8:12 NIV)

WRITE *Your* STORY

Words of Life

I've challenged you to read my story and to let it change your life. God desires us to be free and live in victory! The designs of the enemy will not detour you from your promising future. Don't let the enemy of your past keep you stuck in your yesterday. It's time to live! Doing so is a choice only you can make. Using *Better than Yesterday* proverbs as a guide, what's your story?

The Challenge

1. **The Message**

_____

_____

_____

_____

_____

2. **Words of Life**

_____

_____

_____

_____

_____

3. **The Challenge**

_____

_____

_____

_____

_____

4. **Checkpoints**

_____

_____

_____

_____